I dedicate this book to my beautiful wife Elisa.

Your strength is an inspiration to me.

To my children Luis Alejandro, Manuel Enrique and Elisa Cristina.

You are the beat of my heart

And to my parents in Heaven

Acknowledgments

I want to give special thanks to my son Manuel who inspired me to write this book, my brother Bruce for his unconditional help, Matthew Ellis for proof reading and editing.

I am especially grateful to God, for my life, my health, my family and for always providing us what we need.

Introduction

Sales Revenue is the heart and soul of a company and it is one of the most critical elements in any company's success. We all know that if your company has a steadily declining sales pattern, is like having a death sentence stamped on its forehead. Nobody will invest nor buy into your business. I even venture to say that a company with flat sales is not "surviving" but is reality suffering a slow and painful death because nothing else stays flat over time, such as salaries, product costs, or administrative expenses.

Given the importance of growing sales, then, there may be nothing more challenging than building a successful sales team that will enable winning everyday battles in the marketplace and putting the company in a leadership role. That's the principle intent of this work – to help establish guidelines and actions that will help the reader to create a top-flight sales team and move it to the point of maximum productivity.

Technology has dramatically knocked down entry barriers and we find ourselves in an increasingly competitive environment. Amazon provides the perfect technology platform and logistics backbone needed to start selling almost any product that you can think of by dramatically lowering the entry barriers and fixed costs. Virtually anybody with the right contacts and a computer can launch their own distribution company with almost no start-up costs.

With the availability of an incredible amount of information; purchasing managers and consumers are allowed to find an almost infinite number of different options. Moreover, technology has made the world smaller, oftentimes eliminating city, state, and country boundaries.

All these elements combined work to create a very complex and challenging selling environment. On top of that, if you add social media, spam phone calls, junk emails and the slow disappearance of paper (eg; snail-mail, orders, invoices, etc) nowadays is extremely difficult to cut through the clutter and reach your prospective customers.

In this book, we will try to address the How-To questions for building a highly effective sales team, based primarily on the:

- selling process itself,
- selling techniques, and
- tools needed to make it happen

The definition of madness is to send out a sales team in today's world, without the right strategy, with no proper training, and without the proper tools. It is like sending a soldier to the front line of the battle with no other weapon than a slingshot while your enemy has a machine gun.

CONTENTS

1) Selling Process
    a. Product Definition
    b. Who is My Customer?
    c. Building Constructive Tension
    d. Value Proposition
    e. Prospecting
    f. Setting Up Appointments
    g. Closing the Sale
2) Important Components of an Effective Sales Team
    a. Training
    b. Marketing Tools
    c. Customer Relationship Management (CRM)
    d. Negotiation Skills
3) Building a Motivated Sales Team
    a. Choosing the Right Candidates
    b. Sales Commission
    c. Communication
    d. Empowerment
    e. Building a Lean, Customer-Oriented Organization

1) **The Selling Process**
   a) **Product Definition**

   Starting the selling process with product definition seems a little counterintuitive, but it is not. All selling processes start with having a deep understanding of exactly what we sell and what are our capabilities. A product is the "something" offered for sale. A product can be a service or a good. It can be physical or in a virtual or cyber form. Every product is made at a cost and each is sold at a price. For some companies this information is crystal clear, for others, it is not. Let me put a quick example to illustrate what I mean with this:

   > Let's go over an example. Assume maybe a roofing company, they install new roofs, thus product definition is straight forward: roof installation. In your mind is easy to picture what is exactly this company does. On the other hand, let's think about a more complex product or service. The other day I looked for a company that sells and installs surveillance systems. I found a local company that installs surveillance cameras and they also install phone systems, computer networks, alarm systems, fire alarm systems, and access control systems. In my mind, it was so confusing so I asked myself what is exactly that this company is really selling. Is it security systems? Is it installations? Is the equipment? Is it software? If I hire them tomorrow to install a surveillance system in my company, how would I measure whether they could do a good job, or would my needs be something out of their comfort zone?

   Therefore, it is really important that you as the seller can define clearly what are you selling, your capabilities, and your strengths. We can't just go out there in today's world and say that we do everything and throw a million things to the wall and see what will "stick". Have you ever been to a restaurant that has like a million items on the menu? You probably think to yourself that there is no way that every single item on the menu is good, as a matter of fact your first question to the waitress will be: What's good here? In the same way, maybe you shouldn't pretend that you can possibly be good at everything. Everybody is good at something and that should be your core product and main focus.

A good product needs to be relevant: the users must have an immediate use for it. A product needs to be functionally able to do what it is supposed to do, and then do it with good quality. Quality in the correct definition is the ability that a product has to satisfy the needs of a customer. Users and potential users must know why they need to use it, what benefits they can derive from it, and why your product will be the best good or service for the customer. The knowledge you gain from your own analysis and evaluation may be critical to your customer so as to help them to better understand their own needs.

Finally, your product should be adaptable with trends, time, and changes in needs or technologies. The product should lend itself to adaptation to maintain its own relevance and maintain its future revenue stream. This is done primarily thru research and development. Nobody can survive today's world without a continuous effort to improve your product and make it better.

b) Who is My Customer?

Who is your customer? What are his duties? In what way does your product solve his problems? What benefits will your solution bring him? By what emotions is he driven at everyday work? What makes him feel satisfied and what makes him feel stressed? How to reach out to him? Who is a decision-maker and who are your advocates?

If you cannot answer these questions yet, that's bad – both for you and for your whole team. Understanding your customers' needs is the basis for effective sales. Whichever product you offer, you need to remember that people do not buy functions, shapes, products, or services. To find customers, we need to find out who and where customers are, and to get there, it has to do a lot with my product and strengths. At a first glance, it seems very simple but when we take a closer look, we may find many different types of customers with very diverse needs and we realize that we can't serve all the customers at the same time with the same product. So the definition of the product and the identification of my customers are processes that almost go hand in hand. Let's go back to our first example, the "simple one" the roofer:

> Your product is to install a new roof, now we have different customers: Residential Homeowners, Commercial Building owners, Residential construction companies, Commercial construction companies, banks, and Insurance companies. These can be considered as "market segments". All these customers, that can be a potential client for a new roof, have very different needs and very different priorities. It is important that we study the needs of each different market segment and identify our strengths and choose the specific market segment that we want to concentrate our efforts to grow our sales based on our ability to satisfy the needs of a specific market segment. The same way that a successful restaurant might put in the menu only a handful of dishes that they know they have mastered, and they are the best and then go look for customers that more likely would love the entrees in the menu. Sometimes this process can be completely opposite, we simply choose the customer based on unserved market and low competition, and then we develop our products and capabilities to serve that specific market niche. In the end, the result is the same: laser focus on specific products that serve a particular market segment.

To have a perfect definition of your customer, you need to define firstly, its environment, which includes corporate customers, business partners, distributors, competition, and processes.

Secondly, we need a definition of the business process connected with our product like new customer acquisition, opportunities handling, customer retention, and support, cooperation with partners and distributors, and problems.

Finally and most important is the definition of the customer needs, what do they think and feel, what do they say and do, what do they hear, what do they see, and most importantly, what are your customer's pains and what do they gain by using your product.

c) **Building Constructive Tension**

There is nothing worse than show up to an appointment with a customer and talk about the benefits or the characteristics of a product. Normally the customer loses interest in the first 3-5 minutes.

On the other hand, traditional sales heavily rely on building strong relationships between your outside sales and your customer. But building strong relationships takes a lot of time and effort and not always guarantees success. There is a sales technique developed by Matthew Dixon and Brent Adamson product of years of research that actually put the outside salespeople in control of the conversation and the selling process and it is called the Challenger Sales.

I'll put an example between using a challenger approach versus traditional selling of benefits and features:

> NTN, a very large bearing manufacturer, has a mounted bearing called the Sentinel Bearing. This product was great for the food processing manufacturing plant. One common mistake of some of the salespeople make is going to these places and simply talking about the product: It has stainless steel housing with a stainless steel ball-bearing insert with a solid lube. The solid lube is a polymer that once it heats up, it will bleed the oil and lubricate the rolling elements and when it cools down, the polymer will reabsorb the oil. The bearing insert has a triple lip seal that avoids any contamination of the bearing blah blah blah who cares??? I don't see any applicability for me!
>
> So how should we sell this product then?

Let's start with the specific product: Sentinel (Mounted Ball Bearing). Who is the customer? Food processing plants. They have many conveyors that require mounted bearings that constantly have to be washed down. What are the needs of my customer? First, we need to put ourselves in the shoes of the maintenance manager and operations manager. We really need to have a clear understanding and careful study of our customer's needs. In this case, food processing plants usually run on low margins, it is a steady high volume industry. Uptime is the key. Downtime is extremely expensive for them. Maintenance managers run the maintenance department on a thin budget with a limited number of people, very long hours, and several shifts. In the food industry, the average downtime cost per hour can go from $1,000 to $20,000 so 8 hours of downtime can represent hundreds of thousands of lost revenue. On the other hand, we want to maintain product safety, we don't want that the food or beverages that we produced create any health issue to our customers which by the way that can be extremely expensive for the company if anything like this happens. Also, penalties imposed by food inspections can be very hefty as well. Also, we want to maintain a safe environment for the workers as well, so if grease gets on the floor and a worker slips and falls due to that, then you have possible lawsuits or worker's compensation related expenses, etc.

So how do we get from here to build interest to the customer in my product? The key is to make aware to the customer, problems that they didn't know they have or they were simply not aware of them. This process is called "Constructive Tension". It is called like that because we want the customer make uncomfortable with his current situation, make him aware that he has a problem, so in this case, you need to start asking the right questions to the customer, for example:

How often are you changing the bearings? How often lubricate the bearings? Once a week, once a month? How long does it

take you to lubricate those bearings? How much food-grade grease do you use? How much does the food-grade grease cost you? How often are the conveyors washed down? What is the cost of downtime in your plant is? If your customer doesn't know these facts, then you can share with him the cost of downtime in similar plants in the US, and the cost of the food-grade grease per pound and introduce some facts that they are not aware of, for example: Do you know that the food-grade grease is soluble in water so they got easily washed down when you clean the conveyors? Did you know that when you over grease the bearings, 2 things happen, the seals are compromised so the water and other contaminants get in the rolling elements and also when you have excess grease, the balls don't roll, but slide, and when you do this you significantly reduce bearing life? Do you know that most new bearings come with regular grease and this grease is incompatible with food-grade grease? Then you can introduce some facts like how the excess of grease can create a hazardous situation for workers, how can bleeding grease can get to the product and contaminate the product, how these practices reduce significantly bearing life and you can do simple math on how much this is costing him, in downtime, labor, lubrication cost, etc. Now you got the customer's full attention. He is interested and engaged.

This sales technique requires number one, deep knowledge of the industry, and the customer's business. Secondly, it requires that your outside sales do more active listening and learn to ask the right questions to the customer, instead of trying to just talk about the product. Finally, the approach of the conversation has to be tailored to the person and the function of the person in the organization, touching the "painful" elements of this person executing this function in this organization.

You may think that this technique can be used only in highly engineered products and not with commodities or other types of products, but just think for a minute what kind of advantages or benefits a company like Coca-Cola can offer to a small restaurant in a downtown location. The prestige of the brand along with the demand of the product represents an unquestionable attractiveness for the restaurant.

d) Value Proposition

So far, you have built a constructive tension. You have made the customer aware of issues that he didn't know he had, and you made him uncomfortable with his current situation. Now it is time to be the savior, to present the big solution: Your solution. Let's go back to our example.

> The customer is aware that he is spending too much (considering downtime and labor cost) in lubricating and replacing bearings and at the same time, is creating an unsafe environment for the customers and their workers. It is important at this point trying to quantify with monetary values his unseen cost.
>
> Then we present our solution: Our Sentinel bearing line: You don't have to lubricate the bearing ever again, so you save big time in downtime, labor, and cost of lubrication. You don't have to worry about under or over lubricating the bearing and what is best, you can wash down the bearing and nothing will come in or out of it. So you create a safer environment for your customer, your workers, and in the process, you will double the life of your bearings. At this point, it is extremely important to show the total benefit using the product and demonstrate the customer the total savings and the return of his/her investment by buying your product and how this product will relieve his pain.

Therefore, on the value proposition stage, you need to present the customer how your product is going to fulfill their needs and solve the problems that he/she was not fully aware of.

This stage is extremely important as number one, as it takes away the conversation of price, secondly, it set the basis of a mutual benefit successful negotiation, and finally, it builds a very strong loyalty frame.

Your company will be steering away from those very volatile issues like price and relationship building, and setting up the basis of a strong long term business relationship.

e) **Prospecting**

Prospecting is the first step in the sales process, which consists of identifying potential customers. The goal of prospecting is to develop a database of likely customers and then systematically communicate with them in the hopes of converting them from potential customers to current customers.

Prospecting is one of the most difficult parts of the selling process. As a matter of fact, 42% of outside people have reported that they seriously struggle with prospecting for a new customer. The most common excuse is that they don't have time for prospecting and looking for new customers that they are always trying to catch up with the daily demands of their current customers. Some companies run their outside sales group really thin while other areas in the companies are fully staffed and these companies wonder why they can't grow their business.

We live in a dynamic world. The only constant in this world is that the world continuously changes. So it is expected that your customer basis changes as well: New products, competition gaining ground, customer declining line of business, a customer going out of business, etc . Thus, it is very normal that we lose some customers so in order to keep our sales growth, our new customer inflow rate has to be higher than our lose business rate at all times, and the only way of bringing in a new customer is constantly prospecting new customers by every single one of your outside salespeople in your organization.

So far, you have defined the general market that you are serving, what your product is, and what the value position of your product is. It is time now to identify, based on the customer's needs that your product or service best serves, a market niche. Let's go back to our example.

> We are serving a general industrial replacement market in power transmission. Our products is bearings but we have a specific product that solves a very specific problem in the food industry, so we look at all food-related plants, which include beverages, candies, chocolate, chewing gum and from there we narrow it down, we narrow our search to only food processing plants. We can still narrow our search further to exclusively meat processing plants and vegetable packaging plants (tomatoes, lettuce, etc) that require a higher sanitation grade than other plants.

So our next step is to identify those companies and their locations. We have several "free" online tools. Google is a very powerful tool to get company names by geographic area. A simple google map search, something like Chicken processing plants in Alabama, will give you a list of actual locations with address and phone numbers. There are also other free search directories like Thomas Industrial and Manta. There are also very powerful paid databases like D&B, Data.com, uscompanylist.com, Crunchbase, Zoominfo, etc, that can help to do target searches in a specific SIC code company but will also provide you with contact names, phone numbers, address, and email address.

Another great way to reach a large number of prospects is through trade shows. However, trade shows are very expensive, when you add the cost of booths, hotel, meals, and airplane tickets.

The second part of the prospecting process is to identify who is your specific customer within those organizations, is it the maintenance manager, or purchasing, or the production manager? Maybe the safety manager or top management of the company. Sometimes you need a guerrilla attack strategy on the customer and attack them at different flanks, presenting to each of them how your product can make their life better from their perspective, for example, a safety manager will be interested in knowing that with your bearing there is not going to be any grease on the floor that can potentially create a safety hazard. Sometimes, we need also to think out of the box and contact those areas that apparently have nothing to do with your product.

For example, I was once faced with the challenge of selling an innovative substitute product to a large original equipment manufacturer but engineering has no interest in the product. It was costly and represented a risk for them. Their current setup has worked for years with no issues whatsoever. I contacted the aftermarket part sales department and presented a value proposition of the product based on potential sales in the future for parts replacement and how this product will benefit them and drive more aftermarket sales than their current product. The aftermarket sales group really liked the idea and became my best allies in my effort, pushing engineering for a change of design using our product.

f) **Setting Up Appointments**

There is nothing more difficult and that produces more anxiety than the process of calling a total stranger to set up an appointment. It seems contradictory in the communications era of computers and smartphones that it is extremely hard to reach our prospects and set up appointments. Unfortunately, there is an overflow of telemarketers calls and junk mail. A lot of them are even deceiving and fraudulent so there is a natural reaction of the people simply not to answer a phone number or an email from somebody or a company that he/she doesn't know. We send emails and leave a voicemail and nobody answers you back or calls you back. Sometimes, when you reach somebody, they get angry and rude on the phone. Still, we have a job to do, so what do we do to overcome this? On our sales team, this produces a lot of anxiety. The fear of rejection is natural in all of us. As human beings, we have a strong need to be accepted. The anxiety, this fear, is the main reason why we fail in the first place to constantly generate new business. A natural behavior of your outside sales team is to babysit current customers and pamper them but this behavior won't take your company to the next level and as I mentioned before, without the generation of new revenue and new customers, there is no growth and a company with no growth is just "surviving".

I would say that the first step in cold prospecting is to have the right mindset and the right attitude. We need to get rid of all fears and anger and have a very positive attitude towards the call. Somebody can argue that it is easier to say than done because of the reaction of your prospects to your unsolicited phone call but you have to think that it is not personal; this has nothing to do with you or your company, and you may have reacted the same way if you were in their shoes. The second step of the phone call is to be prepared, to have a written script if possible of what you are going to say. It is very important to set rules of what to say and what not to say.

Be respectful and formal. Properly introduce yourself and your company. Ask the customer if he is familiar with your company and doing a very brief introduction of what you do.

State why you are calling. If your intention is to get an appointment in person, say so.

Do a brief description of the problems you are trying to solve and why your product will fit. Something that will catch their attention and prompt them to hear more.

Set the day and time of the appointment. This is key because most of the time, even if the customer has a genuine interest if you leave it open to the customer, it will never happen thus the best approach is to be proactive and give the customer a day and time and work your appointment from them, having alternative days and times, working your calendar.

Thank them for the opportunity and set up an electronic reminder of the appointment in Outlook or similar.

Most of the time all you are going to get is a voicemail. A simple voicemail won't cut it to get your call returned. You need to leave an attention-catching brief value proposition along with the statement that you will call again. Sometimes, persistence pays off. Obviously, there is a very thin line that divides persistence with being annoying so a balance is important. Sometimes, you can get a particular person that you want to contact from your prospect account but doesn't mean that you should stop there. Try different people and different departments adjusting your value proposition according to the person's responsibilities within the organization.

g) **Closing the Sale**

Every outside salesperson has his/her own strengths in a particular phase of the sales cycle. Some are great at prospecting; some are fantastic in setting up appointments, as they are naturally charming and have no fear of rejection whatsoever. Others are great in presenting to the customer the value proposition and adapting the message depending on the audience. But one particular area where most people struggle is actually closing the sales. So let's review, so far, you have prospected your potential customer, set up the appointment, met with the customer, presented you value proposition based on your products strengths to solve customer problems that they were not even aware of it. So you got this, right? Well not so fast. Sometimes you get really lucky and you get the sales right away, but most of the time, it takes a lot of effort and time to get the customer even to place the first purchase order. Sometimes the inertia, especially if your customer is a large corporation, is too big and changes are a difficult and a slow process. Sometimes a decision has to pass several layers of approvals before the change is actually made. The key here is seven words: Persistence and follow up, follow up, follow up. Most outside salespeople get easily discouraged at the first sign of difficulties in their paths. Change, especially for innovative industrial products, can take many years to take place. Management can get anxious and push for results for short term results, getting all frustrated and aggravating outside salespeople by the constant demand for results. On the other hand, you have the risk of wearing out and annoying your customer to the point that they don't want to deal with you anymore. The key element in the equation is to understand the overall sales cycle, what is involved and how long it takes to close a new business opportunity from the moment of the initial contact, to the reception of the first order. This way everybody understands that this is not a sprint race, it is a marathon and we need to train and be prepared for it.

The second key aspect of closing a new business opportunity is to follow up. As I mentioned before, people often get easily discouraged by difficulties. One important aspect to remember is that no one, not even the most skillful sales representative in the world, will have a 100% success rate. Like baseball, we rely on "batting average" instead. Understand what the win success rate in the industry is and use it in your company as a benchmark. This way both management and the outside salespeople don't have unrealistic expectations of the number of opportunity wins versus the number of new opportunities generated. A reasonable number in general is a 33% success rate. This number may change depending on the industry, the product you are selling, and your company itself. The most important thing is to properly record this information and use your own number based on your experience. Then, when everyone is aligned on the real probability of getting the business, how long it is going to take to get it, and what we need to do. After that, all we have to do is to follow up, follow up, and follow up. We don't dare to throw a number but we are pretty sure that a significant number of opportunities are lost because of the lack of follow up. Customers get busy with other things and our project may be in the back burner and they simply forget. Most of the time, your customer will thank you for reminding him/her about it. But again, we need a balance; we can't overwhelm or annoy our customers. How can we find that fine balance? Communication is key, so after every sales call, it is important to always ask for the next step and the time frame for that next step, what your customer needs to do internally. An outside salesperson should never leave a customer without setting up or knowing what the next step of the opportunity is. It is very important that all this information is properly documented.

2) Important Components of an Effective Sales Team

A) Training

Your sales are the blood, the life of your organization. Without sales, you are dead. When companies have opened outside sales spots, they get desperate not only to fulfill those spots but to have them working fully in the field as quickly as possible. Thus, it is a very common practice to hire salespeople, give them a quick 2-week introduction (sometimes less or sometimes none) and throw them out there in the field. Then top management complains about the poor performance of them and demands a change, a more aggressive team. I wonder whose fault that is.

I strongly believe that the minimum that an outside salesperson needs to spend in training is 4 weeks before going out on his own. Expect at least 6 months to a year for an outside salesperson to be 100% in his game in a territory.

The first phase of the training is learning about the company, internal process, benefits, learn how the company is organized, the procedures, who are your teammates, resources available, etc. This can be from 1 week to several weeks depending on the size of the company.

The second phase is to learn about the product, how the product is manufactured, technical specifications, learn about the competition, and your current customers. Also, it is extremely important that your outside sales know and understand your value proposition. Moreover, the knowledge of the industry and to learn what your customer doesn't know is a huge competitive edge. This requires that the company develops a general knowledge database that continues to be updated and growing. Research and development, market research, and product testing need to be added to the equation as well to help to keep this knowledge base current and relevant. It is important that this product and industry knowledge becomes a collective input from all different areas of the company, including production, research, and development, engineering, marketing, and sales. They all need to feed into this collective knowledge that needs to be shared and taught to all outside salespeople in the organization. Depending on the amount of technical knowledge about the products and knowledge of the industry, this could be from 1 week to 2 or more weeks.

The third phase of the training is learning about selling techniques. The best way to do this is that the new guy spends at least one week with one seasoned outside salesperson. Ideally, the new outside sales should spend 4 weeks working not only with one but several of the outside salespeople so that they can learn from different styles. This way, they can pin up the recent knowledge acquired about the company, the selling process, and the product and industry.

So far, your new outside salesperson has spent almost 2 months in training and yet he/she has not made the first sale. Now it is the time to start going out there in the field. In the final phase of the training, he/she needs to first learn about the territory, the customers, who they are, where they are, how often they need to see them, learning about their different personalities, past problems, old opportunities, current opportunities in the territory, and a potential prospect that has been identified in the past. In the next 6 months, it is extremely important that the manager coaches him/her and get him/her properly introduced to different accounts. This can take from 6 to 8 months to complete, depending on the size of the territory.

B) Marketing Tools

b.1) Advertising

Advertising can take many forms: printed ads, brochures, catalogs, point of sale display, radio ads, and television ads. You can spend as much or as little as you want. Advertising is seen most of the time as an expense, which from the accounting point of view is correct, but in reality, it is a necessary investment for your company. As a general rule, it is recommended to spend at least about 3% of your sales or projected sales on advertising. Your company can't rely 100% on word of mouth, even though it is free and since it relies on other customer experiences which makes its credibility much higher, it is way too slow and has a potential risk: negative reviews travel 10 times faster than positive ones. If you recognize that no human being is perfect thus no company is perfect either, we are prompted, sooner or later, to make mistakes so no company or person has zero negative reviews.

There is no doubt that advertising is very expensive and it is hard to measure its results. We live in the era of information and people get overwhelmed with the amount of information that is bombarded to them every single day; thus you have about 5 seconds to get your message across. So your first priority is to establish clearly the objective of your advertising. Are you trying to build name recognition to your brand, are you trying to generate leads, or are you trying to get your message across?

The second aspect of your advertising is being clear on who do you want to reach. The design of your ad needs to tailor not only the audience you want to reach, but also use the media that is going to reach your target customer more effectively.

Finally, you need to build the message. I see very often how companies waste their resources with ads that simply are meaningless to the customer. I'll give you an example

> Supposed that you have a well-recognized brand, and you have a very innovative product that replaces the chain on your bike. You are trying to reach the end-users to generate "pull" from them. In one ad you simply show the product and its features. In the other, you show a biker, broken down the road with his hand full of grease, trying to fix his bike. Which one do you think it is going to catch your end-user's attention? One that simply describes the product? Or the One that shows them a problem that they can relate with?

Brochures: For most outside sales, having printed quality material is more than a psychological tool than an actual effective tool. You can argue that most of the product literature ends up forgotten in a pile of paper or in the trash can, however, for the outside sales, it is important to have something to show to the customer, something to leave behind. Most people are more visual than auditory so for most customers to have something to feel, see, grab, and touch helps them to see and comprehend what is being said. For this reason, you need to have product samples, (if applicable and/or you are not selling services) to leave or at least to show to the customer.

Public Relationship: There are also cheaper ways to get your message across as well. One is a public relationship and the other is social media. A public relationship is extremely important. It has higher credibility than paid advertising, and aligns well with your overall sales strategy, especially if you have something to teach your customer, something to show them. The participation of industry associations allows you to meet top executives of the most prestigious companies in the industry. On these industry association meetings and trade shows, it is the perfect opportunity to be a guest speaker and talk about sensible problems that your product can solve. Also, at the trade shows, it is perfect to display your product, generate interest and actual potential sales leads to your outside sales group.

Social Media: Social media is a very powerful, cheap advertising alternative available. Don't underestimate the power of social media. It is important to have an active presence on LinkedIn, Facebook, Instagram, Twitter; etc. Social medial helps to accelerate word of mouth advertising quicker than normally it would. But Social Media can be a double edged sword, especially if it is flooded with negative reviews about your product or your company thus it is extremely important to constantly monitor comments and reviews about your product and your company. Social media can be used to publish articles about problems that your customers are not fully aware of and you are trying to teach them to construct constructive tension.

b.2) Price

One of the most controversial subjects in any company is the pricing issues. In a lot of companies pricing is a function of financing which they become the "watchdogs" and the "protectors" of the company's profit. It becomes an internal "war" of us versus them. For finance people, outside sales are trying to ruin the company. Finance sees this sometimes as a game of power and they like to keep the information and the control. In my opinion, going to this path is the start of a company's death.

Let's start by saying that profit is an overall responsibility and a result of team work. Everyone should understand that the company needs to make money to survive and it is everybody's responsibility to increase the profitability of the company thus the cost information, far from putting the company in a vulnerable spot in front of the competition, makes everyone aware of the situation and work together in improving the margins and helping the company because the company's success is my success.

Secondly, pricing is and always has been a 100% marketing function. The pricing of our products has to line up with the market. It is not uncommon seeing a market leader company that keeps steadily increasing prices, year after year, watching strictly supply and demand curves, cost, and profits. They eventually and unintendedly create a huge market for low-cost products / low margin products and all of a sudden, the supply and demand curve drastically changed and lost a huge chunk of market share.

The traditional way of pricing based on cost is an outdated way of pricing your products and services. Price is in direct relationship with the market and the competition. Sometimes it is truly a challenge to price a product, like if it is a new product or service. When you get to truly innovating products like the first computer or the first smartphone, it is truly hard to know how much the customer is going to be willing to pay. It has to do with 100% the total benefit that this customer is going to obtain from the product versus the cost.

Two companies or a company and an individual (called the supplier and the customer) need to be seen as what it truly is: two individuals or entities coming together because there is a mutual benefit by doing so. On one hand you have an individual or company with a specific need and there is a benefit or a gain by satisfying this need. On the other hand, you have your company that is providing this product or service that satisfies this specific individual or company need and you are expecting a benefit from this, a gain or profit by doing so. This mutual gain by the two entities coming together in this transaction we are going to call it "the pie".

On one hand, the price that the purchaser would pay can't be more than the net gain or perceived benefit resulted from satisfying the specific need and, on the other hand, the net gain or benefit of the seller can't be zero or less than zero. Thus the price of the product should be somewhere between these two set points.

So let's see a simple example. Let's say that you are selling a product called "Bueno" that last 3 times longer than the product the customer is using, product "Averaje". Let's suppose that the product "Averaje" costs $10. The net benefit of the customer buying your product is $30. Supposed that the cost of producing your product "Bueno" is $9. In this case, the pie is defined as $30-$9= $21. If the price is $30, it will be indifferent to the customer going with the product from the competition "Averaje" or your product "Bueno". On the other hand, if your company sells the product "Bueno" at $9 will be indifferent to sell or no to sell, because there is no gain or benefit. Moreover, if your product costs more than $30, then your product makes them lose money, and on the other hand, selling below $9, your company will be losing money and those will be business models that at a glance won't make sense. Thus, the price of the product "Bueno" should be between $30 and $9.

It is extremely important to your outside sales to understand this value and keep this in mind when selling to a customer because most of the times they need to explain this value to the customer. Obviously, life is far more complicated than the example I presented, as you have money value of time, opportunity cost, labor cost, downtime cost, etc. so it is hard sometimes to quantify the total benefit that your customer is going to get by switching to your product, but it doesn't mean it is impossible and needs to be done.

b.3) Promotions

Promotion is one of those things that if it is used too much, it has lost its effectiveness, like the retail store that has permanent "discounted" prices. Price promotion and discounts is a great tool when it is used along with a marketing campaign, the launching of a new product or to incentivize the customer to try your product. Your promotion has to be closely tied with a specific objective.

One of the biggest mistakes that most companies make is not to correctly track these sales promotions or special discounts. Promotions are a part of the marketing budget and needs to be accounted as such in your expenses.

Some sales organization has a tendency of thinking that everything is about the price, and constantly begging for price "reductions" to get the business. You need to avoid falling in the trap at all cost. If we price our product correctly based in the market, and your outside sales is capable of delivering the value added proposition of the products and the benefits that the customer will get from your product, price should be last on the list of worries. As I mentioned before, everyone in the organizations needs to be involved and protecting the companies margins.

One of the biggest pitfalls is when you have the business already and you give your customer discounts. Let me illustrate the consequences of giving up margins to your customer:

Suppose that you sell 100 units of your product at $10 each and your cost is $5, so you have a healthy 50% margin. Your net profit with the customer is $500. The competition comes and offers an inferior product at $9. Your customer's purchaser will pressure our outside sales: Company B is offering me the same for $9 and if you don't match the price, I will switch the business. The outside sales enter in panic mode and ask for a discount. Let see what happens if we give the discount: You are giving a 10% discount, right so naturally you think that you will have to increase your volume by 10% to overcome the loss of revenue. In this case, now instead of making net profit of $500, I am making $400 ($4 margin per unit) so I need to overcome $100 of net profit. If I sell them now 10% more units at the discounted price, that's 10 units x $4 = $40, wait a minute, where is the rest? So in this example, the overcome the $100 lost in profit I need to sell additional 250 units with the new margin, that's a whopping 25% increase in volume

Thus price reductions of current business have an exponential effect on the revenue volume needed to overcome the lost profit. Something to really think about when discounting the price to a customer. This is why everyone in the organization needs to understand the importance of protecting the company's profits. Also, the problem of giving up on price is that once you start this path, there is no stop. Your customers will always demand for more and there is always somebody cheaper than you. This is so important to the overall offerings needs to be focused on the value proposition to be sustainable over time, and not on price alone.

b.4) Market Research

As I mentioned before, one huge part of the business intelligence and building a solid and compelling value proposition is based on the knowledge of the industry. This database is constructed in part with market research. It is important that companies spend time and resources in learning about the customers, the competition, and the trends of the market. Here is a list of questions that any company at any given time should be able to respond: What is your market share? What is your market share in a specific market niche? How big is your competition? What are your strengths, weakness, opportunities and threats? What are your customers saying about your product and your company? How is your compensation plan for your outside sales compared with the rest of industry? Is the overall market growing and at what rate? Is the market mature? What are the future expectations of the overall market? Are there potential new competitors either from other industries or different geographical market that can penetrate our market?

b.5) Lead Generation

We talked about how difficult the process of cold calling is for an outside salesperson. There is a huge rejection from customers to be "bothered" by a total estranger. Human beings like to be accepted. During teenager years, it is more evident than ever. In a self-preservation instinct, a lot of outside sales people completely reject the idea of cold calling, even though you can train them and explain them that it is a necessary evil to keep generating new sales and keep growing and you should never take it personally and tune out those rejections. Still success rate is very small. The best thing that any company can do to support this process is put a formal process of lead generation.

There are several ways to generate these sales leads:

Trade shows. This is one of the most traditional and effective ways to generate leads. On trade shows, you show your capabilities to a group of end users walking thru the show. Tradeshows are very expensive, but the leads generated are gold. It is extremely important to follow up those leads

Marketing Campaigns. All marketing ads and efforts should be directed to created pull from the end user and recollect information from those end users that shows interest in your product. Technology nowadays allows, even for printed ads, to have like a scan-able code that can be scanned with your phone and takes you directly to fill out an online form.

Social Media. Contact thru social media can be tricky and can felt like a privacy invasion, however, this is done on a daily basis by many companies. I think that the most effective way to use Social Media is creating relevant technical articles related to the industry that are rather informative than commercial and let it open to the customer to contact you if he/she wants more information about it. That gives you the perfect opportunity to generate a sales lead.

Email Blast. Email address generated by some of the contact databases available, can generate some valuable leads. However, respond rate from emails is very low, but that doesn't mean that we don't try it as it is extremely cheap and simple to do. The secret is not to attach anything to the email in the first place. Just be simple, direct, that can be relevant and incentivize the customer to respond.

Specialized Lead generation companies. There are companies like Oppminner that specializes in lead generation. They can call hundreds of different companies, using a predetermined script and generate hundreds of validated sales leads. Third party companies doing your sales lead generation can be extremely expensive but its quality is the best of all.

Specialized inside sales teams. Some companies found it cheaper to have a group of specialized inside sales team that all they do is generating sales leads. It is no different than using third party companies; expect that you can train them really well in your product and the script. You have far more control and 100% attention.

Of all the tools needed to actually keep a very healthy flow of new opportunities in your company is the lead generation tools that you use. However, without proper follow up, all this effort is wasted. It is important make the outside sales accountable for these leads. And this will bring us to our next subject

C) Customer Relationship Management (CRM).

CRM systems are one of the most loved tools for top managers and the most hated tools for outside sales people. The reason is simple: it is truly big investment for any size company and for the most part the investment is truly worth it, thus most managers want to squeeze it and get as much as they can from it. They love the reports and what they can get from it so they demand more and more and more and for that you need to input more and more and more data. But this input comes at a big cost, outside sales end up spending endless hours doing repetitive boring computer work. At the end, you get what you ask, garbage in, garbage out and a bunch of sales people wasting their time in a computer instead of spending time in the field selling.

Customer Relationship Management Systems area fantastic tool but we need to understand its main purpose and never lose sight of it. The main purpose of a CRM system is a tool designed to help the outside sales to manage opportunities. It is imperative that number one, all sales leads need to be input by marketing and inside sales team and assigned to right person. Then, outside sales are responsible to call and qualify the sales leads and input as much information as they can about the opportunity and the account. The outside sales is responsible to describe in the system about what the opportunity is all about, who are the main contacts of the account, when did they meet, what they discussed, what is the next step. We should be able to attach to the opportunity related documents, request for quotes, quotes, technical documents, etc. We can and should setup dates and reminders, attach emails, anything and everything related to the particular opportunity. This serve primarily as an organizational tool for the outside sales as it help him to keep all information about the opportunity in a single place and help him to properly follow up the opportunity. This needs to be clearly explained to the outside sales group and the importance for them to use the tool. For the managers, it helps them to see if each outside sales person has a "healthy" number of opportunities in the pipeline, how effective or valuable are our sales leads in term of conversion to opportunities, how long our guys are taking to respond to these sales leads. It can be also as a predictor of our sales growth based the dollar amount of the opportunities in the pipeline, considering about a 33% success rate based on the average in the industry in general. It also provides great opportunities for coaching and for evaluating the performance of your outside sales people. The manager and anybody in the organization can access the database and inform themselves about the details of certain opportunity, download important documents, or even upload important documents.

However, the usefulness of a CRM system goes beyond that, it is a tool that helps new hires to quickly catch up with the pending opportunities of his new territory and get all information about the accounts in his territory along with contacts names, emails, phone numbers, etc.

Moreover, CRM can and should be used to eliminate manual and tedious process, like a request for quote, set up of special rebates. Also it can be used to get sales reports so that the status of an account at any given time, it is at the outside sales person finger tips.

But there are many pitfalls involved in a CRM system:

- Asking to fill out way to many details about the outside sales daily activity. CRM will become the most hated tool for all your outside sales people.
- Use opportunity values in the CRM to either bonuses or to punish an outside sell will result in highly inflated values, very far from the real true, giving a false sense of a positive outcome in the future.
- Using CRM to do everything but following up opportunities thus foregoing the most important value that a CRM system brings.

D) Negotiation Skills

There is a huge cloud that darkens the whole sales profession and that is, for most people, they see sales as somebody trying to take advantage of the other, that there is a winner and a loser. There is nothing that it is farther than the true than this statement. The sales process is when two entities that come together to exchange goods or services and both benefit from the exchange. I will put a good "stone age" example.

> Suppose that I am a Native American 1800 years ago. I am great at fishing but I don't know how to make a teepee but there is this other person, that builds great teepees but he doesn't know how to fish. Well, it is obvious then that we come together to exchange goods looking for our own benefit, x number of fishes for a Teepee.

Nowadays, this exchange has been replaced by money to make it more universal and facilitate the exchange but the principle is the same: Both companies is looking for a benefit, one has a specific need, and the other one can satisfy that need and by doing so is expecting a reward or a compensation. Thus in every single sale transaction, what is really happening is a negotiation were parties will benefit from an exchange of good or services. As I mentioned before, we are going to call this total benefit that resulted from these two entities coming together "the pie" and this whole combined benefit of this two entities coming together is what is out for negotiation. It doesn't serve any good to Walmart if they drive all their suppliers out of business and vice versa, if all suppliers confabulate to drive Walmart out of business it doesn't help them either.

Taking these facts into consideration, all your outside sales people needs to understand that every single sale is a negotiation process where both companies will benefit from it. This is why it is so important that clearly learn about your value proposition and what is your company is bringing to the table and at the end, they need to constantly pursue the balance point where both companies are benefiting from the business relationship.

It is the company's management duty to provide the negotiation skills necessary to its entire outside sales group.

There are thousands of books and advanced courses in negotiation and this book doesn't even dare to pretend to be a source for it, but I would like to go over a few key concepts relating to negotiation.

The Pie: Supposed that a company is 10 times bigger than its supplier. The supplier is providing a new product that will save them $1,000 in electricity and the cost of producing this item is $100. Thus the Pie, the mutual benefit is $900. The bigger company can argue, I am ten times bigger than you and claim that benefit in proportion to its size, but based on that, the bigger company is simply "bullying" the smaller company. The correct way will be to equally divide the pie 50-50, thus the supplier should make an argument of selling the product for $550 ($450+100).

Principle of the Divided Cloth: The 2,000-year-old Babylonian Talmud forms the basis for Jewish civil, criminal and religious law. Among its principles, it introduces a new form or a different form of negotiation. The best way to explain this principle is with an example. Suppose that two people are disputing a piece of fabric and the fabric is 100 yards long. Subject A says that he is entitled to 50 yards while the subject B says that he is entitled to the whole fabric (100 yards). The principle establishes that then subject A will receive 25 yards of the fabric while subject B should get 75 yards. This seems very counterintuitive but basically, the principle will split equally what is in dispute that is 50 yards as subject A already conceded to subject B half of the fabric. Let's go back then to our example and see how this principle applies to this case. Suppose that the supplier wants the whole pie for themselves and wants to charge $1,000 for the product but then the customer says, no, I am not going to pay more than $500 for the service. Then, applying the principle of the divided cloth, the amount in dispute is $500 and this is what we will try to negotiate as the customer already conceded $500, so if we divide equally the disputed amount, then what we charge for the service is $750.

Let me give a real-life example. I had a large client that told me that they are currently paying $12 for the product. Based on our cost and our value proposition our quote came as $18 per unit. The customer wanted to give us the business but they said that $18 was too much, that the maximum they would pay was $14. I came back and I applied this principle and negotiated with them. What I did at that moment is to ask them to meet me "half way", which is $16. The customer accepted my proposed price and the felt it was fair. As you may see, based on this principle, the "cloth" was the difference between $12 and $18 but the part in "dispute" was really between $18 and $14, hence $16 was the fair price.

Never say no: Suppose that you are trying to get new business and your customer says that they accept your price and they are happy with the quality of the product, but they request consignment inventory in their warehouse, in other words, they want you to pay for the financial cost of carrying an inventory. You analyze the situation and take into account your margins, your opportunity cost of money, and labor cost to administrate the remote inventory at the customer's warehouse; you realize you will be losing money if you accept this deal. But instead of going back keep and telling the customer no, there is no deal, you just go back to the customer with an out of the box solution and a different proposition offer where both can benefit. The customer has given you the opportunity to do business, so don't waste it and negotiate your way in.

3) Building a Motivated Sales Team

a) Choosing the Right Candidates

Hiring new employees is a costly process. The average US cost to hire a new employee is $4,000 and it takes averages 45 days to fill in the position. We have put a lot of emphasis on the importance of the training of outside sales and how long it takes for him/her to be 100% productive in his/her territory. For outside sales, the cost of a new outside salesperson can be around $80,000 per year. For this reason, it is extremely important to avoid at all costs turn over in your outside sales group.

The first step is choosing the right candidate is developing an "ideal profile" of what we think our outside sales should have in terms of experience, personality, and skills. The skills and experience needed will be defined by the type of product that you are selling. The more technical and complex the product you are selling, the higher skills levels needed thus, skills should clearly outweigh the experience of the candidate and vice versa, the more commodity or less technical the product is, the lower the skills needed and the more emphasis we put in experience as knowledge of the market is more important than the skills.

Personality is, in my opinion, one of the most important elements in the hiring process, and most of the time is completely overlooked.

A great outside sale has an entrepreneurship spirit. They are passionate about hunting prospects and normally think outside the box. They are goal oriented and relentless in the pursue of their objectives.

One of the most valuable treats of an effective outside sales is their capacity to follow up every step of the selling process so organization skills and attention to details are also very important.

A good salesperson constantly is learning, searching constantly for knowledge of the product and the industry. As he/she gains more knowledge, his/her capacity to challenge the customer and the probability of breaking the status quo increases
But, perhaps one of the most important personality characteristics of an outstanding salesperson is empathy and humility. I was once mucked by

a recruiter when a said in an interview that one of my most important attributes as a salesperson is that I am a "good Christian". Believe or not, an outstanding outside salesperson is always there to help the customer, has humility and recognizes mistakes, doesn't lie and never hides. On the contrary a great outside salesperson always faces the problem, no matter how hard and tough it is. Most customers recognize that everybody makes mistakes. What makes a difference between a poor service and a great service is the capacity to recover from those mistakes.

So, when choosing the right candidate, you need a combination of experience, with education and personality. Thinking that you will find the ideal candidate with the perfect combination of personality, skills, and experience is very naïve. Companies need to find a balance and make concessions when choosing a candidate or otherwise they can be years before they find their perfect candidate.
So in situations when you can't find candidates with the right experience, my advice is go for the "diamond in the rough", choose the candidate with the right education and the ideal personality

b) Sales Commissions

Let's talk about what everybody doesn't want to talk about: Money. Having the right type of remuneration is extremely important for employee retention. We already spoke about how expensive employee turnover is and the cost of hiring a new employee, especially in sales thus the craft of the right remuneration package needs to be carefully designed with this objective in mind.

There are a few things that you need to take into account in your commission plan for your outside sales.

First of all, let's talk about Price's Law. Derek Price, who was a British physicist, historian of science, and information scientist, discovered something about his peers in academia. He noticed that there were always a handful of people who dominated the publications within a subject.

Price found out the following (now called Price's law): 50% of the work is done by the square root of the total number of people who participate in the work.

So if your company has 9 outside sales, 3 outside sales will bring 50% of the revenue. If you have 25 people in your outside sales force, 5 should bring in 50% of the sales. As the number of people grows, the percentage of your top performers keeps reducing and reducing. If you don't believe me, just take your real estate agents working in the county you live; if there are 500 real estate agents, 22 will sell 50% of the total Real State sales on the area, that's only 5%, and see how many houses were sold in your area and how many those top 5% real estate agents sold. I bet that you will be stunned and quickly realize that next time you need to sell your house, you need to use one of those top 5% agents.

So this is a reality no matter what you do, there are always going to be superstars in your team and a big majority that just do okay. So don't get crazy or mad about it, don't try to change the world, and don't try to re-arrange territories or anything like that, just accept it and embrace it.

Your plan has to consider those superstars and reward them well enough so that they will never leave your company. They will be your prima donnas and a lot of people in your organization will hate them and they will see them as arrogant and a pain in their rear end. Remember that one of the traits of top performers is empathy for your customer's needs and they will go the extra mile to help the customer and they will fight the internal battles to make it happen and that will bring friction with some of the internal people.

The worst you can ever do is to consider that "these guys are making too much money" and consider cutting their commission. If you do that, they are going to leave and they are plenty of companies out there willing to pay extra for those top performers.

Secondly, your commission can't have a ceiling; again, if you put a ceiling, the message you are sending to your top performers is, I don't care how good you are, this is how much I am going to pay you. Not a good message to send to your top performers. You see, the other trait that your top performers have is to have an entrepreneurial spirit and there is nothing closer to having your own business as working as an outside salesperson and having unlimited earning potential. At the end, if they win big, you will win big as well.

Finally, what is the ideal combination of fixed salary versus commission? There is no easy answer and it will depend on the nature of your business. I'll give you a great example. Motion Industries, headquartered in Birmingham, Alabama, is a distributor of industrial parts and has 300,000 customers and annual sales of $6.53 billion. Motion is one of the largest MRO suppliers in the world and their success in my opinion has a lot to do with their outside sales group. Motion is a sales-oriented organization and they barely have turnover within the outside sales group. The reason: their commission plan. Their outside salespeople get 100% commission based on profit margins with no thrills, no fancy salary, and just straight commission with no ceiling either. The end result is that some of their highest performers make past 200K per year. Their bottom performers, they just naturally leave because they don't make enough. The payment structure attracts top entrepreneurship minded people. I also love the idea of focusing on the profits and not sales. Focusing on the bottom line and avoid overly aggressive tactics on getting unprofitable business sends a crystal clear message: I make money, then you make money, the more I make, the more you make, thus we are partners. What a beauty!!!

Again a big warning: trying to "level" commission earnings across the outside salespeople is a terrible idea; your top performers will leave and only the mediocre ones will stay. Once I worked for a company that paid a 70% fixed salary and 30% sales commission but the commission rate was "adjusted down" as your numbers grew, so why even bother?

However, this 100% commission may not work well on highly technical sales or sales where there is a very long selling cycle. As a general rule, the longer and more technical and difficult is the sale, the higher the proportion of fixed salary needs to be, and the shorter the sales cycle is; the higher proportion of sales commission needs to be incorporated. This way, the outside salesperson is constantly rewarded for his/her daily effort.

Also, some companies incorporate bonuses in their payment structure. Bonuses are nice for team accomplishments as an addition to the commission but should never replace sales commission itself for two reasons: they normally have a ceiling and secondly, the target may be too high to accomplish and won't create the desired behavior we want in our outside sales group.

c) Communication

Most outside salespeople spend most of their time completely disconnected from the company office, especially in bigger nationwide companies. This makes your outside salespeople kind of the "lone wolves" out there. In one hand, outside salespeople feel that nobody cares about them and they are "facing the world" by themselves with very little support; and in the other hand, people in the office may think that outside sales are spoiled people that they have a bad arrogant attitude and all they do is complain and play golf in the afternoon. These extreme cases cause a profound dissociation of the sales group with the rest of the organization.

Communication between outside salespeople and the rest of the organization is extremely important. A company should set the basis of favorable and constant communication between the different departments and the sales organization. Common objectives, mission, vision, and values should be clearly transmitted at all levels so everyone works together toward a common goal. I have been faced in my career with a price group controlling quotes to a customer, guardians of the profit, completely disconnected and unaware on how the sales process within the company works, and vice versa, and outside sales groups with a complete disconnection of margins, cost, margin objectives, etc...

This lack of communication and common goal setting set the table for a constant and painful battle between sides where there are no possible winners.

Moreover, it is extremely important communication flows both ways like a two-way street. Not only do you need to clearly communicate all strategy, mission, and vision, but also that the organization needs to hear the sales group, complaints, opinions, and ideas and take them seriously. On surveys done in most organizations, this is the number one complaint of the outside salespeople: Their voice is not heard.

d) Empowerment

Traditional organizations often have many management levels and a lot of rules and procedures in an effort to strictly control behavior and prevent "mistakes". Employees get themselves submerged on a sea of bureaucracy within the organization. The message that these organizations send is loud and clear: Employees are the source of problems and they are a burden. This type of mentality kills creativity and takes away focus on the customer. How often have you encounter a problem in a store and then you feel extremely frustrated to be "bounced" around to different people and never find anybody with authority to help you to resolve it? How often does a salesperson throw you "sorry it's company policy there is nothing I can do" and he/she is incapable of thinking outside the box and looking at the big picture?

When your outside salespeople are incapable of making decisions on their own, then the speed of response becomes slow and you are putting the decision in the hands of somebody who doesn't have direct contact with the customer and doesn't have to face the customer hence, the decision he/she will make will negatively impact our relationship with the customer.

I am not saying that the company should not have rules or procedures, without them, it would be no consistency in performance and it would be chaos. What I am saying basically is that there are certain decisions that the outside salespeople need to be empowered to make within certain guidelines from the company. To be effective, the outside salesperson needs to be properly trained and well informed about the company objectives, situation, and procedures. Good examples of the kind of issues that the outside sales should be empowered to make, as they deal with these issues almost on a daily basis, are prices, discounts, returns, expedite orders, quality issues, free samples, and account opening decisions. Again, complete freedom can't be allowed but decisions under specific procedures and guidelines can be a powerful element for the company to gain light speed, very necessary in today's hectic and competitive world.

Empowerment also implies to listen to the employee, to listen to their suggestion and implement changes. Remember that a company is no more than a group of people working together. In a genuine team, the whole is much bigger than the sum of the parts, thus a world-class company should truly value each individual employee's input and encourage their participation. Normally, the satisfaction levels of the world-class companies that highly regard each individual employee are extremely high as this is one of the most basic human needs: Every human being needs to belong, that they are appreciated and they are making a contribution. This is the heart of empowerment; recognize that every single employee is important, that they are not dumb, that they are perfectly capable of making decisions on their own for the good of the whole group.

e) **Building a Lean, Customer-Oriented Organization**

Lean Six Sigma organizations' primary focus is the customer. Everything that doesn't add value from the customer's perspective is considered waste. If you think about it, there are a millions of procedures, and forms and rules that from the customer perspective, don't add value. All bureaucracy and paperwork should be minimized. From the six sigma perspective, every single process in the company can be subject to be improved. Empowerment and Lean organizations go hand to hand. It is important to create multidisciplinary groups in the organization, dedicated to improving every single process on a continuous basis. To be able to accomplish that, every single employee should be trained in the continuous improvement tools and get six sigma certification, including your outside salespeople who very often get completely ignored as they are perceived that they are "out in the field"/. As I said before, one of the biggest problems most companies faces is the lack of attachment that the outside sales people have for the company, that they feel they are lone rangers out there. There is no better way to bring them home and make them feel that they really belong and they are important is by making them part of continuous improvement initiatives. Sure, there are always going to be some negative people saying that it is a waste of time for them, but it will be a true waste of time if the changes are not made and they are not truly listening. One of the key elements in continuous improvement groups is that nobody can dominate the discussion and people in power positions within the company, should step down and get on the same level as every employee participating in the group.

Also, lean organizations are flatter, which means fewer management levels which allow better communication and less bureaucracy. In modern customer-oriented companies, employees are the organization's greatest resource and they are empowered to take decisions on their own in an effort to quickly address customer's problems and better serve their needs. The results are often exponential, because as employees in Lean Six Sigma organizations feel more motivated, their productivity levels greatly increase.

www.ingramcontent.com/pod-product-compliance
Lightning Source LLC
Chambersburg PA
CBHW050319220526
45465CB00005B/2054